Fix-It and Forget-It

Best
5-INGREDIENT
Comfort Food Recipes

75 QUICK & EASY SLOW COOKER MEALS

HOPE COMERFORD

Photos by Bonnie Matthews

Good Books

New York, New York

Copyright © 2020 by Good Books
Photos by Bonnie Matthews

Good Books books may be purchased in bulk at special discounts for sales promotion, corporate gifts, fund-raising, or educational purposes. Special editions can also be created to specifications. For details, contact the Special Sales Department, Good Books, 307 West 36th Street, 11th Floor, New York, NY 10018 or info@skyhorsepublishing.com.

Good Books is an imprint of Skyhorse Publishing, Inc.®, a Delaware corporation.

Visit our website at www.goodbooks.com.

10 9 8 7 6 5 4 3 2 1

Library of Congress Cataloging-in-Publication Data is available on file.

Cover design by Abigail Gehring
Cover photo by Getty Images

Print ISBN: 978-1-68099-475-9
Ebook ISBN: 978-1-68099-479-7

Printed in China

Table of Contents

Welcome to Fix-It and Forget-It Best 5-Ingredient Comfort Food Recipes

When you know you have a busy day, week, or month ahead, finding something to cook can be a daunting task. So many recipes call for so many ingredients, and let's face it, you don't have the time or energy for that! That's why you've purchased this copy of *Fix-It and Forget-It Best 5-Ingredient Comfort Food Recipes*. This cookbook is here to help maximize your time and take away the dread of figuring out what you're going to make to eat when you're at your busiest. We've chosen 75 of the best 5-Ingredient recipes for this cookbook, all of which have been tested by real home cooks, like you, to bring fuss-free food to your table more quickly.

What Qualifies as a 5-Ingredient Recipe?

- A recipe that has 5 or fewer ingredients.
- Spices do not count.
- Water does not count.
- *Optional* ingredients do not count.
- Serving suggestion items, such as rice or pasta, do not count.

Choosing a Slow Cooker

Not all slow cookers are created equal . . . or work equally well for everyone!

Those of us who use slow cookers frequently know we have our own preferences when it comes to which slow cooker we choose to use. For instance, I love my programmable slow cooker, but there are many programmable slow cookers I've tried that I've strongly disliked. Why? Because some go by increments of 15 or 30 minutes and some go by 4, 6, 8, or 10 hours. I dislike those restrictions, but I have family and friends who don't mind them at all! I am also pretty brand loyal when it comes to my manual slow cookers, because I've had great success with those and have had unsuccessful moments with slow cookers of other brands. So, which slow cooker(s) is/are best for your household?

It really depends on how many people you're feeding and if you're gone for long periods of time. Here are my recommendations:

For 2–3 person household	3–5 quart slow cooker
For 4–5 person household	5–6 quart slow cooker
For a 6+ person household	6½–7 quart slow cooker

Large slow cooker advantages/disadvantages:

Advantages:

- You can fit a loaf pan or a baking dish into a 6- or 7-quart, depending on the shape of your cooker. That allows you to make bread or cakes, or even smaller quantities of main dishes. (Take your favorite baking dish and loaf pan along when you shop for a cooker to make sure they'll fit inside.)
- You can feed large groups of people, or make larger quantities of food, allowing for leftovers, or meals, to freeze.

Disadvantages:
- They take up more storage room.
- They don't fit as neatly into a dishwasher.
- If your crock isn't ⅔–¾ full, you may burn your food.

Small slow cooker advantages/disadvantages:

Advantages:
- They're great for lots of appetizers, for serving hot drinks, for baking cakes straight in the crock, and for dorm rooms or apartments.
- Great option for making recipes of smaller quantities.

Disadvantages:
- Food in smaller quantities tends to cook more quickly than larger amounts. So keep an eye on it.
- Chances are, you won't have many leftovers. So, if you like to have leftovers, a smaller slow cooker may not be a good option for you.

My recommendation:

Have at least two slow cookers; one around 3 to 4 quarts and one 6 quarts or larger. A third would be a huge bonus (and a great advantage to your cooking repertoire!). The advantage of having at least a couple is you can make a larger variety of recipes. Also, you can make at least two or three dishes at once for a whole meal.

Manual versus Programmable

If you are gone for only six to eight hours a day, a manual slow cooker might be just fine for you. If you are gone for more than eight hours during the day, I would highly recommend purchasing a programmable slow cooker that will switch to warm when the cook time you set is up. It will allow you to cook a wider variety of recipes.

The two I use most frequently are my 4-quart manual slow cooker and my 6½-quart programmable slow cooker. I like that I can make smaller portions in my 4-quart slow cooker on days I don't need or want leftovers, but I also love how my 6½-quart slow cooker can accommodate whole chickens, turkey breasts, hams, or big batches of soups. I use them both often.

Get to know your slow cooker . . .

Plan a little time to get acquainted with your slow cooker. Each slow cooker has its own personality—just like your oven (and your car). Plus, many new slow cookers cook hotter and faster than earlier models. I think that with all of the concern for food safety, the slow-cooker manufacturers have amped up their settings so that "High," "Low," and "Warm" are all higher temperatures than in the older models. That means they cook hotter—and therefore, faster— than the first slow cookers. The beauty of these little machines is that they're supposed to cook low and slow. We count on that when we flip the switch in the morning before we leave the house for ten hours or so. So, because none of us knows what kind of temperament our slow cooker has until we try it out, nor how hot it cooks—don't assume anything. Save yourself a disappointment and make the first recipe in your new slow cooker on a day when you're at home. Cook it for the shortest amount of time the recipe calls for. Then, check the food to see if it's done. Or if you start smelling food that seems to be finished, turn off the cooker and rescue your food.

Also, all slow cookers seem to have a "hot spot," which is of great importance to know, especially when baking with your slow cooker. This spot may tend to burn food in that area if you're not careful. If you're baking directly in your slow cooker, I recommend covering the "hot spot" with some foil.

Take notes . . .

Don't be afraid to make notes in your cookbook. It's yours! Chances are, it will eventually get passed down to someone in your family, and they will love and appreciate all of your musings. Take note of which slow cooker you used and exactly how long it took to cook the recipe. The next time you make it, you won't need to try to remember. Apply what you learned to the next recipes you make in your cooker. If another recipe says it needs to cook 7–9 hours, and you've discovered your slow cooker cooks on the faster side, cook that recipe for 6–6½ hours and then check it. You can always cook a recipe longer—but you can't reverse things if it's overdone.

Get creative . . .

If you know your morning is going to be hectic, prepare everything the night before, take it out so the crock warms up to room temperature when you first get up in the morning, then plug it in and turn it on as you're leaving the house.

 If you want to make something that has a short cook time and you're going to be gone longer than that, cook it the night before and refrigerate it for the next day. Warm it up when you get home. Or, cook those recipes on the weekend when you know you'll be home and eat them later in the week.

Slow-Cooking Tips and Tricks and Other Things You May Not Know

* Slow cookers tend to work best when they're ⅔ to ¾ of the way full. You may need to increase the cooking time if you've exceeded that amount, or reduce it if you've put in less than that. If you're going to exceed that limit, it would be best to reduce the recipe, or split it between two slow cookers. (Remember how I suggested owning at least two or three slow cookers?)

- Keep your veggies on the bottom. That puts them in more direct contact with the heat. The fuller your slow cooker, the longer it will take its contents to cook. Also, the more densely packed the cooker's contents are, the longer they will take to cook. And finally, the larger the chunks of meat or vegetables, the more time they will need to cook.

- Keep the lid on! Every time you take a peek, you lose 20 minutes of cooking time. Please take this into consideration each time you lift the lid! I know, some of you can't help yourself and are going to lift anyway. Just don't forget to tack on 20 minutes to your cook time for each time you peeked!

- Sometimes it's beneficial to remove the lid. If you'd like your dish to thicken a bit, take the lid off during the last half hour to hour of cooking time.

- If you have a big slow cooker (7- to 8-quart), you can cook a small batch in it by putting the recipe ingredients into an oven-safe baking dish or baking pan and then placing that into the cooker's crock. First, put a trivet or some metal jar rings on the bottom of the crock, and then set your dish or pan on top of them. Or a loaf pan may "hook on to" the top ridges of the crock belonging to a large oval cooker and hang there straight and securely, "baking" a cake or quick bread. Cover the cooker and flip it on.

- The outside of your slow cooker will be hot! Please remember to keep it out of reach of children and keep that in mind for yourself as well!

- Get yourself a quick-read meat thermometer and use it! This helps remove the question of whether or not your meat is fully cooked, and helps prevent you from overcooking your meat as well.

  Internal Cooking Temperatures:
  - Beef—125–130°F (rare); 140–145°F (medium); 160°F (well-done)
  - Pork—140–145°F (rare); 145–150°F (medium); 160°F (well-done)
  - Turkey and Chicken—165°F
  - Frozen meat: The basic rule of thumb is, don't put frozen meat into the

slow cooker. The meat does not reach the proper internal temperature in time. This especially applies to thick cuts of meat! Proceed with caution!

- Add fresh herbs 10 minutes before the end of the cooking time to maximize their flavor.
- If your recipe calls for cooked pasta, add it 10 minutes before the end of the cooking time if the cooker is on High; 30 minutes before the end of the cooking time if it's on Low. Then the pasta won't get mushy.
- If your recipe calls for sour cream or cream, stir it in 5 minutes before the end of the cooking time. You want it to heat but not boil or simmer.

Approximate Slow-Cooker Temperatures (Remember, each slow cooker is different):

- High—212°F–300°F
- Low—170°F–200°F
- Simmer—185°F
- Warm—165°F

Cooked and dried bean measurements:

- 16-oz. can, drained = about 1¾ cups beans
- 19-oz. can, drained = about 2 cups beans
- 1 lb. dried beans (about 2½ cups) = 5 cups cooked beans

Breakfast

Slow-Cooker Oatmeal

Martha Bender, New Paris, IN

Makes 7–8 servings

Prep Time: 10–15 minutes ⚜ *Cooking Time: 8–9 hours* ⚜ *Ideal slow-cooker size: 4- to 5-qt.*

2 cups rolled oats

4 cups water

1 large apple, peeled and chopped

1 cup raisins

1 tsp. cinnamon

1–2 Tbsp. orange zest

1. Combine all ingredients in your slow cooker.

2. Cover and cook on Low 8–9 hours.

3. Serve topped with brown sugar, if you wish, and milk.

Breakfast Apples

Joyce Bowman, Lady Lake, FL
Jeanette Oberholtzer, Manheim, PA

Makes 4 servings
Prep Time: 10–15 minutes ⚘ *Cooking Time: 2–8 hours* ⚘ *Ideal slow-cooker size: 3-qt.*

4 medium-sized apples, peeled
and sliced

¼ cup honey

1 tsp. cinnamon

2 Tbsp. melted coconut oil

2 cups dry granola cereal

1. Place apples in your slow cooker.

2. Combine remaining ingredients. Sprinkle the mixture evenly over the apples.

3. Cover and cook on Low 6–8 hours, or overnight, or on High 2–3 hours.

4. Serve as a side dish to bacon and bagels, or use as a topping for waffles, French toast, pancakes, or cooked oatmeal.

Slow-Cooker Yogurt

Becky Fixel, Grosse Pointe Farms, MI

Makes 12–14 servings

Prep Time: 2 minutes & Cooking Time: 12–14 hours & Ideal slow-cooker size: 6-qt.

I gallon whole milk

5.3 oz. Greek yogurt with cultures

1. Empty the gallon of whole milk into your slow cooker and put it on High heat for 2–4 hours. Length of time depends on your model, but the milk needs to heat to just below boiling point, about 180–200°F.

2. Turn off your slow cooker and let your milk cool down to 110–115°F. Again, this will take 2–4 hours. Set your starter Greek yogurt out so it can reach room temperature during this step.

3. In a small bowl, add about 1 cup of the warm milk and the Greek yogurt and mix together. Pour the mixture into the milk in the slow cooker and mix it in by stirring back and forth. Replace the lid of your slow cooker and wrap the whole thing in a towel. Let sit for 12–14 hours.

4. After 12 hours check on your glorious yogurt!

5. Line a colander with cheesecloth and place in bowl. Scoop your yogurt inside and let it sit for at least 4 hours. This will help separate the extra whey from the yogurt and thicken your final yogurt.

Tip:

"My yogurt didn't all fit in one colander, but thankfully I had a second one to use. You can wait until the yogurt sinks down and there is more space in the colander if you only have one. Spoon finished yogurt into jars or containers and place in the fridge. After your yogurt is done, you're going to have leftover whey. Put it in a jar and pop it in the fridge. Use it to replace stock in recipes, water your plants, or to make cheese. It's amazing what you can do with it!"

—Becky Fixel

Huevos Rancheros in Crock

Pat Bishop, Bedminster, PA

Makes 6 servings

Prep Time: 25 minutes ⚭ *Cooking Time: 2 hours* ⚭ *Ideal slow-cooker size: 6-qt.*

3 cups salsa, room temperature

2 cups cooked beans, drained, room temperature

6 eggs, room temperature

salt and pepper to taste

⅓ cup reduced-fat grated Mexican blend cheese, optional

1. Mix salsa and beans in the slow cooker.

2. Cook on High for 1 hour or until steaming.

3. With a spoon, make 6 evenly spaced dents in the salsa mixture; try not to expose the bottom of the crock. Break an egg into each dent.

4. Salt and pepper eggs. Sprinkle with cheese if you wish.

5. Cover and continue to cook on High until egg whites are set and yolks are as firm as you like them, approximately 20–40 minutes.

6. To serve, scoop out an egg with some beans and salsa.

Easy Egg and Sausage Puff

Sara Kinsinger
Stuarts Draft, VA

Makes 6 servings
Prep Time: 10–15 minutes ⚶ *Cooking Time: 2–2½ hours* ⚶ *Ideal slow-cooker size: 2- to 4-qt.*

1 lb. loose sausage

6 eggs

1 cup all-purpose baking mix

1 cup shredded cheddar cheese

2 cups milk

¼ tsp. dry mustard, optional

1. Brown sausage in nonstick skillet. Break up chunks of meat as it cooks. Drain.

2. Meanwhile, spray interior of slow cooker with nonstick cooking spray.

3. Mix all ingredients in slow cooker.

4. Cover and cook on High 1 hour. Turn to Low and cook 1–1½ hours, or until the dish is fully cooked in the center.

Layered Breakfast Casserole

Cathy Boshart
Lebanon, PA

Makes 8–10 servings
Prep Time: 30 minutes   Cooling Time: 4–8 hours
Cooking Time: 1 hour   Ideal slow-cooker size: 6-qt.

6 medium-sized potatoes

2 dozen eggs

1 lb. chopped ham

12 oz. Velveeta cheese,
shredded

1. The day before you want to serve the dish, boil the potatoes in their skins until soft. Chill. When thoroughly chilled, grate. Spread in bottom of greased slow cooker.

2. Scramble and cook eggs in a nonstick skillet. When just set, spoon cooked eggs over top of potatoes.

3. Layer ham evenly over eggs. Sprinkle with cheese.

4. Bake on Low for 1 hour or until cheese is melted.

Blueberry Fancy

Leticia A. Zehr
Lowville, NY

Makes 12 servings
Prep Time: 10–15 minutes & Cooking Time: 3-4 hours & Ideal slow-cooker size: 5-qt.

I loaf Italian bread, cubed, divided

I pint blueberries, divided

8 oz. cream cheese, cubed, divided

6 eggs

1½ cups milk

1. Place half the bread cubes in the slow cooker.

2. Drop half the blueberries over top the bread.

3. Sprinkle half the cream cheese cubes over the blueberries.

4. Repeat all 3 layers.

5. In a mixing bowl, whisk together eggs and milk. Pour over all ingredients.

6. Cover and cook on Low until the dish is custardy and set.

7. Serve with maple syrup or blueberry sauce.

Variation:

Add 1 tsp. vanilla to Step 5.

Appetizers & Snacks

Slow-Cooked Salsa

Andy Wagner, Quarryville, PA

Makes 2 cups

Prep Time: 15 minutes ⚘ Cooking Time: 1½–3 hours
Standing Time: 2 hours ⚘ Ideal slow-cooker size: 3-qt.

10 plum tomatoes
2 garlic cloves
1 small onion, cut into wedges
1–2 jalapeños
½ cup chopped fresh cilantro
½ tsp. sea salt, optional

Tip:

Wear disposable gloves when cutting hot peppers; the oils can burn your skin. Avoid touching your face when you've been working with hot peppers.

1. Core tomatoes. Cut a small slit in two tomatoes. Insert a garlic clove into each slit.

2. Place all tomatoes and onions in a 3-qt. slow cooker.

3. Cut stems off jalapeños. (Remove seeds if you want a milder salsa.) Place jalapeños in the slow cooker.

4. Cover and cook on High for 2½–3 hours or until vegetables are softened. Some may brown slightly. Cool at least 2 hours with the lid off.

5. In a blender, combine the tomato mixture, cilantro, and salt if you wish. Cover and process until blended.

6 Refrigerate leftovers.

Serving suggestion:
Garnish with cilantro and jalapeño.

Mexican Dip

Marla Folkerts, Holland, OH

Makes 15 servings
Prep Time: 15–20 minutes ❧ *Cooking Time: 2–3 hours* ❧ *Ideal slow-cooker size: 3-qt.*

1 lb. low-fat ground beef or turkey

8-oz. pkg. grated low-fat Mexican cheese

16-oz. jar mild, thick and chunky picante salsa, or thick and chunky salsa

6-oz. can refried beans

1. Brown meat in nonstick skillet.

2. Place meat and remaining ingredients into your crock and stir.

3. Cover and cook on Low for 3 hours, or until all ingredients are heated through and melted.

Bacon Cheddar Dip

Arlene Snyder
Millerstown, PA

Makes 15 servings
Prep Time: 10–15 minutes ⚶ *Cooking Time: 1½–2 hours* ⚶ *Ideal slow-cooker size: 4-qt.*

2 8-oz. pkgs. cream cheese, softened

2 cups sour cream

1 lb. bacon, fried and crumbled

4 cups shredded cheddar cheese, divided

Tip:
Save a few bacon crumbs to sprinkle on top.

1. In a mixing bowl, beat cream cheese and sour cream until smooth.

2. Fold in bacon and 3 cups cheddar cheese.

3. Place mixture in slow cooker and sprinkle with remaining cheese.

4. Cover and cook on Low 1½–2 hours, or until heated through.

5. Serve with white corn chips.

Artichoke Dip

Colleen Heatwole
Burton, MI

Makes 9–12 servings
Prep Time: 20 minutes   &   Cooking Time: 1–1½ hours   &   Ideal slow-cooker size: 2-qt.

12-oz. jar marinated artichoke
hearts

1 cup grated Parmesan cheese

⅔ cup sour cream

⅔ cup mayonnaise

2 Tbsp. diced pimento

1. Drain artichoke hearts very well. Chop finely.

2. Place chopped artichokes in slow cooker. Combine with remaining ingredients.

3. Cover and cook on Low 1–1½ hours, stirring occasionally.

4. Serve with tortilla chips.

Apricot Butter

Janet L. Roggie, Lowville, NY

Makes 15 cups
Prep Time: 10 minutes & *Cooking Time: 8 hours* & *Ideal slow-cooker size: 5-qt.*

4 28-oz. cans apricots, drained
3 cups sugar
2 tsp. cinnamon
½ tsp. ground cloves
2 Tbsp. lemon juice

1. Puree fruit in food processor. Pour into slow cooker.

2. Stir in remaining ingredients.

3. Cover and cook on Low 8 hours.

4. Pour into hot, sterilized 1-cup, or 1-pt., jars and process according to standard canning methods.

5. Serve as a spread with bread, or as a sauce with pork or chicken dishes.

Rhonda's Apple Butter

Rhonda Burgoon, Collingswood, NJ

Makes 24 servings (2 Tbsp. each)
Prep Time: 20 minutes ❧ *Cooking Time: 12–14 hours* ❧ *Ideal slow-cooker size: 3-qt.*

4 lbs. apples
2 tsp. cinnamon
½ tsp. ground cloves

1. Peel, core, and slice apples. Place in the slow cooker.

2. Cover. Cook on High 2–3 hours. Reduce to low and cook 8 hours. Apples should be a rich brown and be cooked down by half.

3. Stir in spices. Cook on High 2–3 hours with lid off. Stir until smooth.

4. Pour into freezer containers and freeze, or pour into sterilized jars and seal.

Soups, Stews & Chilis

Black Bean Soup

Dorothy VanDeest, Memphis, TN

Makes 8 servings

Prep Time: 10 minutes to precook beans & Cooking Time: 6½–8½ hours & Ideal slow-cooker size: 4-qt.

1 lb. dried black beans

9 cups water

3 cups water

¼ lb. bacon, fried crisp and crumbled, or ½ lb. smoked ham, chopped

2 medium-sized onions, chopped

1 tsp. garlic salt

¼ tsp. coarsely ground pepper

1. Place dried beans in large stockpot. Cover with 9 cups water. Cover pot and bring to a boil.

2. Boil 10 minutes. Reduce heat and simmer, covered, for 1½ hours, or until beans are tender. Discard cooking water.

3. Combine cooked beans, 3 cups water, bacon, onions, garlic salt, and pepper in slow cooker, stirring well.

4. Cover and cook on High 4–6 hours.

Tip:

To serve beans as a side dish, add a 4-oz. can of chopped green chilies, 1 tsp. powdered cumin, and 1/4 tsp. dried oregano to 5-6 cups of fully cooked beans. Simmer for 25 minutes to blend flavors.

—Bonita Ensenberger
Albuquerque, NM

Old-Fashioned Bean Soup

Shirley Sears
Sarasota, FL

Makes 8–10 servings
Prep Time: 10 minutes ❧ *Cooking Time: 5-12 hours* ❧ *Ideal slow-cooker size: 4- to 5-qt.*

1 lb. dried navy beans, soaked overnight

16 cups water, divided

1 lb. meaty ham bones, or ham pieces

1 tsp. salt

½ tsp. pepper

½ cup chopped celery leaves

1 medium onion, chopped

1 bay leaf, optional

1. Place dried beans and 8 cups water in a large stockpot. Cover and allow to soak for 8 hours or overnight. Drain.

2. Place soaked beans and 8 cups fresh water in your slow cooker.

3. Add all remaining ingredients.

4. Cover and cook on Low 10–12 hours, or on High 5–6 hours, or until the meat is falling off the bone and the beans are tender but not mushy.

Split Pea Soup with Ham

Elena Yoder
Carlsbad, NM

Makes 8 servings
Prep Time: 15 minutes ❧ *Cooking Time: 4 hours* ❧ *Ideal slow-cooker size: 4-qt.*

2½ qts. water

I ham hock or pieces of cut-up ham

2½ cups split peas, dried

I medium onion, chopped

3 medium carrots, cut in small pieces

salt and pepper to taste

1. Bring water to a boil in a saucepan on your stovetop.

2. Place all other ingredients into slow cooker. Add water and stir together well.

3. Cover and cook on High for 4 hours, or until vegetables are tender.

4. If you've cooked a ham hock, remove it from the soup and de-bone the meat. Stir cut-up chunks of meat back into the soup before serving.

Hearty Lentil and Sausage Stew

Cindy Krestynick
Glen Lyon, PA

Makes 6 servings
Prep Time: 5–10 minutes ⚜ *Cooking Time: 4–6 hours* ⚜ *Ideal slow-cooker size: 6-qt.*

2 cups dry lentils, picked over and rinsed

1½-oz. can diced tomatoes

8 cups canned chicken broth, or water

1 Tbsp. salt

½–1 lb. pork or beef sausage, cut into 2-inch pieces

1. Place lentils, tomatoes, chicken broth, and salt in slow cooker. Stir to combine. Place sausage pieces on top.

2. Cover and cook on Low 4–6 hours, or until lentils are tender but not dry or mushy.

Pork Potato Stew

Kristin Tice
Shipshewana, IN

Makes 4 servings
Prep Time: 20 minutes & Cooking Time: 4 hours & Ideal slow-cooker size: 3-qt.

1 lb. ground pork

½ cup chopped onion

1 sweet potato, cubed and
peeled, approximately 3 cups

2 beef bouillon cubes

½ tsp. dried rosemary

3 cups water

1. Place meat and onion in nonstick skillet. Brown on stovetop.

2. Place drained meat, along with onion, into slow cooker. Add remaining ingredients.

3. Cover and cook on Low for 4 hours.

Variation:

Add a bit of hot sauce to make the soup spicy, or serve on the side to accommodate those who don't like hot food.

Beef Barley Soup

Stacie Skelly
Millersville, PA

Makes 8–10 servings

Prep Time: 15 minutes   Cooking Time: 9¼ –11½ hours   Ideal slow-cooker size: 6-qt.

3–4-lb. chuck roast

2 cups chopped carrots

6 cups vegetable, or tomato, juice, divided

2 cups quick-cook barley

water, to desired consistency

salt and pepper to taste, optional

1. Place roast, carrots, and 4 cups juice in slow cooker.

2. Cover and cook on Low 8–10 hours.

3. Remove roast. Place on platter and cover with foil to keep warm.

4. Meanwhile, add barley to slow cooker. Stir well. Turn heat to High and cook 45 minutes to 1 hour, until barley is tender.

5. While barley is cooking, cut meat into bite-sized pieces.

6. When barley is tender, return chopped beef to slow cooker. Add 2 cups juice, water if you wish, and salt and pepper, if you want. Cook for 30 minutes on High, or until soup is heated through.

Beef Vegetable Soup

Margaret Moffitt
Bartlett, TN

Makes 12 servings
Prep Time: 15 minutes ⚹ *Cooking Time: 6–8 hours* ⚹ *Ideal slow-cooker size: 4-qt.*

1 lb. chunks of stewing beef

28-oz. can stewed tomatoes, undrained

1 tomato can of water

16-oz. pkg. of your favorite frozen vegetable

half a 10-oz. pkg. frozen chopped onions

1½ tsp. salt and ¼–½ tsp. pepper

2 Tbsp. chopped fresh parsley, optional

1. Combine all ingredients in slow cooker.

2. Cover and cook on High 6–8 hours.

Navy Bean and Ham Soup

Jennifer Freed, Rockingham, VA

Makes 6 servings
Prep Time: overnight, or approximately 8 hours   &   Cooking Time: 8–10 hours
Ideal slow-cooker size: 6½- or 7-qt.

6 cups water

5 cups dried navy beans, soaked overnight, drained, and rinsed

1 pound ham, cubed

15-oz. can corn, drained

4-oz. can mild diced green chiles, drained

1 onion, diced, optional

salt and pepper to taste

1. Place all ingredients in the slow cooker.

2. Cover and cook on Low 8–10 hours, or until beans are tender.

Succulent Beef Stew

Linda Thomas, Sayner, WI

Makes 6 servings
Prep Time: 30 minutes ⚓ *Cooking Time: 8 hours* ⚓ *Ideal slow-cooker size: 3-qt.*

1–1½ lbs. stew meat

1 medium to large onion, chopped

salt and pepper, optional

1¾ cups low-sodium beef broth

1 broth can of water

5 shakes Worcestershire sauce, optional

2 bay leaves, optional

½ lb. baby carrots

5 medium white potatoes, peeled or unpeeled, cut into ½-inch chunks

1. In a nonstick skillet, brown stew meat and chopped onion. Sprinkle with salt and pepper if you wish. Transfer mixture to the slow cooker.

2. Add broth and water, and Worcestershire sauce and bay leaves if you choose to. Stir together well.

3. Cover and cook on Low 4 hours.

4. Layer in vegetables. Push down into liquid as much as you can. Cover and continue cooking on Low for 4 more hours.

5. If the stew seems to get dry, add ½ cup water.

Chipotle Navy Bean Soup

Rebecca Weybright, Manheim, PA

Makes 6 servings
Prep Time: 10 minutes ❧ Cooking Time: 8 hours
Standing Time: 12 hours ❧ Ideal slow-cooker size: 5-qt.

1½ cups dried navy beans, soaked overnight

1 onion, chopped

1 dried chipotle chile, soaked 10–15 minutes in cold water

4 cups water

1–2 tsp. salt

2 cups canned reduced-sodium tomatoes with juice

1. Drain soaked beans.

2. Add to the slow cooker with onion, chile, and 4 cups water.

3. Cover and cook on Low for 8 hours until beans are creamy.

4. Add salt and tomatoes.

5. Use an immersion blender to puree soup.

Butternut Squash Soup

Elaine Vigoda, Rochester, NY

Makes 4–6 servings

Prep Time: 5 minutes ❧ *Cooking Time: 4–8 hours* ❧ *Ideal slow-cooker size: 4- to 5-qt.*

5½ cups low-sodium chicken broth (use vegetable broth to keep this vegetarian/vegan)

I medium-sized butternut squash, peeled and cubed

I small onion, chopped

I tsp. ground ginger

I tsp. garlic, minced, optional

¼ tsp. nutmeg, optional

1. Place chicken broth and squash in the slow cooker. Add remaining ingredients.

2. Cover and cook on High 4 hours, or on Low 6–8 hours, or until squash is tender.

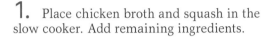

Chili with Two Beans

Patricia Fleischer, Carlisle, PA

Makes 6–8 servings
Prep Time: 15 minutes ❧ *Cooking Time: 4½–5 hours* ❧ *Ideal slow-cooker size: 6-qt.*

I lb. lean ground beef

6-oz. can low-sodium tomato paste

40½-oz. can low-sodium kidney beans, undrained

2 15½-oz. cans low-sodium pinto beans, undrained

2 Tbsp. chili powder

1. Brown beef in large nonstick skillet. Drain.

2. Combine all ingredients in the slow cooker.

3. Cover and cook on Low 4½–5 hours.

Easy Spicy Chili

Becky Gehman, Bergton, VA

Makes 9–12 servings

Prep Time: 15 minutes   ⚜   Cooking Time: 4–10 hours   ⚜   Ideal slow-cooker size: 4- to 5-qt.

2 lbs. lean ground beef

3 15½-oz. cans low-sodium red kidney beans, drained

2–3 14½-oz. cans low-sodium diced tomatoes, undrained

2 onions, chopped

1 green pepper, chopped, optional

2–3 Tbsp. chili powder

1. Brown ground beef in a large nonstick skillet. Drain.

2. Place beef in the slow cooker. Add kidney beans, tomatoes, onions, and green pepper, if you wish, to the cooker. Fold together well.

3. Cover and cook on Low 8–10 hours or on High 4–6 hours.

4. Add chili powder 2 hours before the end of the cooking time.

Tips:

1. This can be successfully frozen and reheated later.

2. You may want to pass salt and pepper as you serve the chili.

3. You may add about 2 Tbsp. of flour along with the chili powder in Step 4 if you want to thicken the chili.

Quick Taco Chicken Soup

Karen Waggoner
Joplin, MO

Makes 4–6 servings
Prep Time: 5 minutes ⚬ *Cooking Time: 1 hour* ⚬ *Ideal slow-cooker size: 4-qt.*

12-oz. can cooked chicken, undrained

14-oz. can chicken broth

16-oz. jar mild thick-and-chunky salsa

15-oz. can ranch-style beans

15-oz. can whole-kernel corn

1. Mix all ingredients in slow cooker.

2. Cover and cook on High 1 hour. Keep warm on Low until ready to serve.

Chicken Rice Soup

Norma Grieser
Clarksville, MI

Makes 8 servings
Prep Time: 30 minutes ♣ *Cooking Time: 4–8 hours* ♣ *Ideal slow-cooker size: 4- to 6-qt.*

4 cups chicken broth

4 cups cut-up chicken, cooked

1⅓ cups cut-up celery

1⅓ cups diced carrots

1 qt. water

1 cup uncooked long-grain rice

1. Put all ingredients in slow cooker.

2. Cover and cook on Low 4–8 hours, or until vegetables are cooked to your liking.

Easy Potato Soup

Yvonne Kauffman Boettger
Harrisonburg, VA

Makes 8 servings
Prep Time: 10 minutes ⚭ *Cooking Time: 5 hours* ⚭ *Ideal slow-cooker size: 4- to 6-qt.*

3 cups chicken broth

2-lb. bag frozen hash brown potatoes

1 ½ tsp. salt

¾ tsp. pepper

3 cups milk

3 cups shredded Monterey Jack, or cheddar, cheese

1. Place chicken broth, potatoes, salt, and pepper in slow cooker.

2. Cover and cook on High 4 hours, or until potatoes are soft.

3. Leaving the broth and potatoes in the slow cooker, mash the potatoes lightly, leaving some larger chunks.

4. Add milk and cheese. Blend in thoroughly.

5. Cover and cook on High until cheese melts and soup is hot.

Main Dishes

Beef

Whole-Dinner Roast Beef

Betty Moore
Plano, IL
Rhonda Freed
Lowville, NY

Makes 6–8 servings
Prep Time: 10 minutes ⚜ *Cooking Time: 8–9 hours* ⚜ *Ideal slow-cooker size: 3½-to 4-qt.*

3–5-lb. beef roast

10¾-oz. can cream of
mushroom soup

1 envelope dry onion soup mix

4 cups baby carrots

4–5 potatoes, quartered

1. Place the roast in your slow cooker.

2. Cover with mushroom soup. Sprinkle with onion soup mix.

3. Cover and cook on Low 6 hours.

4. Add potatoes and carrots, pushing down into the sauce as much as possible.

5. Cover and cook another 2–3 hours, or until vegetables are tender, but meat is not dry.

Roast Beef and Mushrooms

Gladys M. High
Ephrata, PA

Makes 4–6 servings

Prep Time: 10 minutes ⚜ *Cooking Time: 8–10 hours* ⚜ *Ideal slow-cooker size: 3-qt.*

3-lb. boneless chuck roast

¼ lb. fresh mushrooms, sliced, or 4-oz. can mushroom stems and pieces, drained

1 cup water

1 envelope dry brown gravy mix

1 envelope dry Italian dressing mix

1. Place roast in slow cooker.

2. Top with mushrooms.

3. In a small bowl, mix together water, dry gravy mix, and dry Italian dressing mix. Pour over roast and mushrooms.

4. Cover and cook on Low 8–10 hours, or until meat is tender but not dry.

Italian Roast with Potatoes

Ruthie Schiefer, Vassar, MI

Makes 8 servings
Prep Time: 30–35 minutes ⚜ *Cooking Time: 6–7 hours* ⚜ *Ideal slow-cooker size: 5-qt.*

6 medium-sized potatoes, peeled if you wish, and quartered

1 large onion, sliced

3–4-lb. boneless beef roast

26-oz. jar tomato and basil pasta sauce, divided

½ cup water

3 low-sodium beef bouillon cubes

1. Place potatoes and onion in bottom of slow cooker.

2. Meanwhile, brown roast on top and bottom in nonstick skillet.

3. Place roast on top of vegetables. Pour any drippings from the skillet over the beef.

4. Mix 1 cup pasta sauce and ½ cup water together in a small bowl. Stir in bouillon cubes. Spoon mixture over meat.

5. Cover and cook on Low 6–7 hours, or until meat is tender but not dry.

6. Transfer roast and vegetables to serving platter. Cover with foil.

7. Take 1 cup cooking juices from the slow cooker and place in medium-sized saucepan. Stir in remaining pasta sauce. Heat.

8. Slice or cube beef. Pour sauce over the meat and vegetables or serve on the side.

Peppercorn Beef Roast

Stacie Skelly, Millersville, PA

Makes 6–8 servings
Prep Time: 10–15 minutes ⚜ *Cooking Time: 8–10 hours* ⚜ *Ideal slow-cooker size: 4-qt.*

3–4-lb. chuck roast

½ cup reduced-sodium soy sauce or liquid aminos

1 tsp. garlic powder

1 bay leaf

3–4 peppercorns

2 cups water

1 tsp. thyme, optional

1. Place roast in the slow cooker.

2. In a mixing bowl, combine all other ingredients and pour over roast.

3. Cover and cook on Low 8–10 hours.

4. Remove meat to a platter and allow to rest before slicing or shredding.

Tip:

To make gravy to go with the meat, whisk together ½ cup flour and ½ cup water, stir into meat juices in crock, turn cooker to High, and bring cooking juices to a boil until gravy is thickened.

Spicy Beef Roast

Karen Ceneviva, Seymour, CT

Makes 10 servings
Prep Time: 15–20 minutes ⚬ *Cooking Time: 3–8 hours* ⚬ *Ideal slow-cooker size: 4- or 5-qt.*

1–2 Tbsp. cracked black peppercorns

2 cloves garlic, minced

3-lb. eye of round roast, trimmed of fat

3 Tbsp. balsamic vinegar

¼ cup reduced-sodium soy sauce or Bragg's liquid aminos

2 Tbsp. Worcestershire sauce

2 tsp. dry mustard

1. Rub cracked pepper and garlic onto roast. Put roast in the slow cooker.

2. Make several shallow slits in top of meat.

3. In a small bowl, combine remaining ingredients. Spoon over meat.

4. Cover and cook on Low for 6–8 hours, or on High for 3–4 hours, just until meat is tender, but not dry.

Pork

Savory Pork Roast

Mary Louise Martin, Boyd, WI

Makes 4–6 servings

Prep Time: 15 minutes ⚶ Cooking Time: 3½–4½ hours ⚶ Ideal slow-cooker size: 6-qt. oval

4-lb. boneless pork butt roast

1 tsp. ground ginger

1 Tbsp. fresh minced rosemary

½ tsp. mace or nutmeg

1 tsp. coarsely ground black pepper

2 tsp. salt

2 cups water

1. Grease interior of slow-cooker crock.

2. Place roast in the slow cooker.

3. In a bowl, mix spices and seasonings together. Sprinkle half on top of roast, pushing down on spices to encourage them to stick.

4. Flip roast and sprinkle with rest of spices, again pushing down to make them stick.

5. Pour 2 cups water around the edge, being careful not to wash spices off meat.

6. Cover. Cook on Low 3½–4½ hours, or until instant-read meat thermometer registers 140°F when stuck into center of roast.

Cranberry Pork Roast

Chris Peterson, Green Bay, WI
Joyce Kaut, Rochester, NY

Makes 6–8 servings
Prep Time: 5 minutes 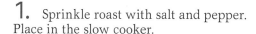 *Cooking Time: 6–8 hours* 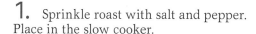 *Ideal slow-cooker size: 5-qt.*

3–4-lb. pork roast

salt and pepper to taste

1 cup finely chopped
cranberries

¼ cup honey

1 tsp. grated orange peel

½ tsp. ground nutmeg, optional

½ tsp. ground cloves, optional

1. Sprinkle roast with salt and pepper. Place in the slow cooker.

2. Combine remaining ingredients in a bowl. Pour over roast.

3. Cover and cook on Low 6–8 hours, or until meat is tender.

Honey Barbecue Pork Chops

Tamara McCarthy
Pennsburg, PA

Makes 8 servings
Prep Time: 15 minutes ⚭ *Cooking Time: 6–8 hours* ⚭ *Ideal slow-cooker size: 4-qt.*

8 pork chops, divided

1 large onion, sliced, divided

1 cup barbecue sauce

⅓ cup honey

1. Place one layer of pork chops in your slow cooker.

2. Arrange a proportionate amount of sliced onions over top.

3. Mix barbecue sauce and honey together in a small bowl. Spoon a proportionate amount of sauce over the chops.

4. Repeat the layers.

5. Cover and cook on Low 3–4 hours.

6. If the sauce barely covers the chops, flip them over at this point. If they're well covered, simply allow them to cook another 3–4 hours on Low, or until they're tender but the meat is not dry.

Pork Chops and Apple Slices

Dorothy VanDeest
Memphis, TN
Dale Peterson
Rapid City, SD

Makes 4 servings

Prep Time: 15 minutes ⚜ *Cooking Time: 6–8 hours* ⚜ *Ideal slow-cooker size: 3- to 4-qt.*

4 pork loin chops, about 1-inch thick, well trimmed

2 medium-sized apples, peeled, cored, and sliced

1 tsp. butter or margarine

¼ tsp. nutmeg, optional

salt and pepper to taste

1. Heat a nonstick skillet until hot. Add chops and brown quickly. Turn and brown on the other side.

2. While chops are browning, place half the sliced apples in the slow cooker. Top with 2 chops. Repeat the layers.

3. Dot with butter and sprinkle with nutmeg. Sprinkle generously with salt and pepper.

4. Cover and cook on Low 6–8 hours, or until meat is tender but not dry.

Raspberry Balsamic Pork Chops

Hope Comerford, Clinton Township, MI

Makes 4–6 servings
Prep Time: 5 minutes & Cooking Time: 7–8 hours & Ideal slow-cooker size: 3-qt.

4–5 lbs. thick-cut pork chops

¼ cup raspberry balsamic vinegar

2 Tbsp. olive oil

½ tsp. kosher salt

½ tsp. garlic powder

¼ tsp. basil

¼ cup water

1. Place pork chops in the slow cooker.

2. In a small bowl, mix together the remaining ingredients. Pour over the pork chops.

3. Cover and cook on Low for 7–8 hours.

Carnitas

Hope Comerford, Clinton Township, MI

Makes 12 servings
Prep Time: 10 minutes ⚓ *Cooking Time: 10–12 hours* ⚓ *Ideal slow-cooker size: 4-qt.*

2-lb. pork shoulder roast

1½ tsp. kosher salt

½ tsp. pepper

2 tsp. cumin

5 cloves garlic, minced

1 tsp. oregano

3 bay leaves

2 cups low-sodium chicken stock

2 Tbsp. lime juice

1 tsp. lime zest

1. Place pork shoulder roast in crock.

2. Mix together the salt, pepper, cumin, garlic, and oregano. Rub it onto the pork roast.

3. Place the bay leaves around the pork roast, then pour in the chicken stock around the roast, being careful not to wash off the spices.

4. Cover and cook on Low for 10–12 hours.

5. Remove the roast with a slotted spoon, as well as the bay leaves. Shred the pork between 2 forks, then replace the shredded pork in the crock and stir.

6. Add the lime juice and lime zest to the crock and stir.

7. Serve on warmed white corn tortillas.

North Carolina Barbecue

J. B. Miller
Indianapolis, IN

Makes 8–12 servings
Prep Time: 15 minutes ❧ *Cooking Time: 5–8 hours* ❧ *Ideal slow-cooker size: 4- to 5-qt.*

3–4-lb. pork loin, roast or shoulder

I cup apple cider vinegar

¼ cup, plus I Tbsp., prepared mustard

¼ cup, plus I Tbsp., Worcestershire sauce

2 tsp. red pepper flakes

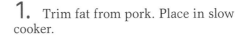

1. Trim fat from pork. Place in slow cooker.

2. In a bowl, mix remaining ingredients together. Spoon over meat.

3. Cover and cook on High 5 hours, or Low 8 hours, or until meat is tender but not dry.

4. Slice, or break meat apart, and serve drizzled with the cooking juices. If you use the meat for sandwiches, you'll have enough for 8–12 sandwiches.

Slow-Cooked Pork Barbecue for a Group

Linda E. Wilcox
Blythewood, SC

Makes 20–24 servings
Prep Time: 15 minutes ⚘ *Cooking Time: 12–14 hours* ⚘ *Ideal slow-cooker size: 6-qt.*

6-lb. pork roast

18-oz. bottle favorite barbecue sauce

2 Tbsp. brown sugar

2 tsp. dry mustard

2 Tbsp. minced onion

1. Place roast in slow cooker and cook on Low 8–10 hours, or until meat is tender but not dry.

2. Remove roast to platter. (Drain drippings and reserve for a soup stock or for a gravy.) Using 2 forks, shred the pork.

3. Return shredded pork to slow cooker and stir in remaining ingredients.

4. Cook on Low 4 hours. Serve on rolls.

Chicken & Turkey

Roast Chicken

Betty Drescher, Quakertown, PA

Makes 6 servings
Prep Time: 30 minutes ⚜ Cooking Time: 9–11 hours ⚜ Ideal slow-cooker size: 4- to 5-qt.

3–4-lb. roasting chicken or hen
1½ tsp. salt
¼ tsp. pepper
1 tsp. parsley flakes, divided
1 Tbsp. olive oil
½–1 cup water

1. Thoroughly wash chicken and pat dry.

2. Sprinkle cavity with salt, pepper, and ½ tsp. parsley flakes. Place in the slow cooker, breast side up.

3. Rub or brush chicken with olive oil.

4. Sprinkle with remaining parsley flakes. Add water around the chicken.

5. Cover and cook on High 1 hour. Turn to Low and cook 8–10 hours.

Tips:

1. Sprinkle with basil or tarragon in Step 4, if you wish.

2. To make it a more complete meal, put carrots, onions, and celery in the bottom of the slow cooker.

Chicken and Rice Casserole

Dale Peterson
Rapid City, SD
Joyce Shackelford
Green Bay, WI

Makes 3–4 servings
Prep Time: 20 minutes ♣ Cooking Time: 4–5 hours ♣ Ideal slow-cooker size: 6-qt.

2 10¾-oz. cans cream of celery soup, divided

2-oz. can sliced mushrooms, undrained

½ cup raw long-grain rice

2 whole boneless, skinless chicken breasts, uncooked and cubed

1 Tbsp. dry onion soup mix

½ soup can water

1. Spray inside of slow cooker with nonstick cooking spray. Combine 1 can of soup, mushrooms, and rice in greased slow cooker. Stir until well blended.

2. Lay chicken on top. Pour 1 can of soup over all.

3. Sprinkle with onion soup mix. Add ½ soup can of water.

4. Cover and cook on Low 4–5 hours, or until both chicken and rice are fully cooked but not dry.

Garlic and Lemon Chicken

Hope Comerford, Clinton Township, MI

Makes 5 servings

Prep Time: 5 minutes ⚓ *Cooking Time: 5–6 hours* ⚓ *Ideal slow-cooker size: 3- or 5-qt.*

4–5 lbs. boneless, skinless chicken breasts or thighs

½ cup minced shallots

½ cup olive oil

¼ cup lemon juice

1 Tbsp. garlic paste (or use 1 medium clove garlic, minced)

1 Tbsp. no-salt seasoning

⅛ tsp. pepper

1. Place chicken in the slow cooker.

2. In a small bowl, mix the remaining ingredients. Pour this mixture over the chicken in the crock.

3. Cover and cook on Low for 5–6 hours.

That's Amore Chicken Cacciatore

Carol Sherwood, Batavia, NY

Makes 6 servings
Prep Time: 20 minutes ❧ *Cooking Time: 7–9 hours* ❧ *Ideal slow-cooker size: 6-qt.*

6 boneless, skinless chicken breast halves, divided

28-oz. jar low-sugar, low-sodium spaghetti sauce

2 green peppers, chopped

1 onion, minced

2 Tbsp. minced garlic

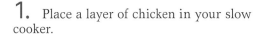

1. Place a layer of chicken in your slow cooker.

2. Mix remaining ingredients together in a bowl. Spoon half of the sauce over the first layer of chicken.

3. Add remaining breast halves. Top with remaining sauce.

4. Cover and cook on Low 7–9 hours, or until chicken is tender but not dry.

Serving Suggestion:
Serve with cooked spaghetti or other pasta.

Thai Chicken

Joanne Good, Wheaton, IL

Makes 6 servings

Prep Time: 5 minutes ⚬ *Cooking Time: 8–9 hours* ⚬ *Ideal slow-cooker size: 4-qt.*

6 skinless chicken thighs

¾ cup salsa, your choice of mild, medium, or hot

¼ cup chunky all-natural peanut butter

1 Tbsp. low-sodium, soy sauce or liquid aminos

2 Tbsp. lime juice

1 tsp. gingerroot, grated, optional

2 Tbsp. chopped cilantro, optional

1 Tbsp. chopped dry-roasted peanuts, optional

1. Put chicken in the slow cooker.

2. In a bowl, mix remaining ingredients together, except cilantro and chopped peanuts.

3. Cover and cook on Low 8–9 hours, or until chicken is cooked through but not dry.

4. Skim off any fat. Remove chicken to a platter and serve topped with sauce. Sprinkle with peanuts and cilantro, if you wish.

5. Serve over cooked rice.

Easy Enchilada Shredded Chicken

Hope Comerford, Clinton Township, MI

Makes 10–14 servings

Prep Time: 5 minutes ⚘ Cooking Time: 5–6 hours ⚘ Ideal slow-cooker size: 3- or 5-qt.

5–6 lbs. boneless, skinless chicken breast

14½-oz. can low-sodium petite diced tomatoes

1 medium onion, chopped

8 oz. red enchilada sauce

½ tsp. salt

½ tsp. chili powder

½ tsp. basil

½ tsp. garlic powder

¼ tsp. pepper

1. Place chicken in the crock.

2. Add in the remaining ingredients.

3. Cover and cook on Low for 5–6 hours.

4. Remove chicken and shred it between two forks. Place the shredded chicken back in the crock and stir to mix in the juices.

Serving suggestion:
Serve over salad, brown rice, quinoa, sweet potatoes, nachos, or soft corn tortillas. Add a dollop of yogurt and a sprinkle of fresh cilantro.

Tender Barbecued Chicken

Mary Lynn Miller
Reinholds, PA

Makes 4–6 servings

Prep Time: 10–15 minutes ♣ *Cooking Time: 8–10 hours* ♣ *Ideal slow-cooker size: 5-qt.*

3–4-lb. broiler/fryer chicken, cut up

1 medium-sized onion, thinly sliced

1 medium-sized lemon, thinly sliced

18-oz. bottle barbecue sauce

¾ cup cola

1. Place chicken in slow cooker. Top with onion and lemon slices.

2. Combine barbecue sauce and cola. Pour over all.

3. Cover and cook on Low 8–10 hours, or until chicken is tender but not dry.

Cranberry Chicken Barbecue

Gladys M. High
Ephrata, PA

Makes 6–8 servings
Prep Time: 10 minutes ⚜ *Cooking Time: 4–8 hours* ⚜ *Ideal slow-cooker size: 4- to 5-qt.*

4 lbs. chicken pieces, divided

½ tsp. salt

¼ tsp. pepper

16-oz. can whole-berry cranberry sauce

1 cup barbecue sauce

½ cup diced celery, optional

½ cup diced onion, optional

1. Place ⅓ of the chicken pieces in the slow cooker.

2. Combine all remaining ingredients in a mixing bowl. Spoon ⅓ of the sauce over the chicken in the cooker.

3. Repeat Steps 1 and 2 twice.

4. Cover and bake on High 4 hours, or on Low 6–8 hours, or until chicken is tender but not dry.

Maple-Glazed Turkey Breast with Rice

Jeanette Oberholtzer
Manheim, PA

Makes 4 servings
Prep Time: 10–15 minutes ⚭ *Cooking Time: 4–6 hours* ⚭ *Ideal slow-cooker size: 3- to 4-qt.*

6-oz. pkg. long-grain wild rice mix

1½ cups water

2-lb. boneless turkey breast, cut into 1½–2-inch chunks

¼ cup maple syrup

1 onion, chopped

¼ tsp. ground cinnamon

½ tsp. salt, optional

1. Combine all ingredients in the slow cooker.

2. Cook on Low 4–6 hours, or until turkey and rice are both tender, but not dry or mushy.

Turkey with Mushroom Sauce

Judi Manos, West Islip, NY

Makes 12 servings
Prep Time: 25 minutes ♣ Cooking Time: 7–8 hours ♣ Ideal slow-cooker size: 6-qt.

I large boneless, skinless turkey breast, halved

2 Tbsp. melted coconut oil

2 Tbsp. dried parsley

½ tsp. dried oregano

½ tsp. kosher salt

¼ tsp. black pepper

½ cup white wine

I cup fresh mushrooms, sliced

2 Tbsp. cornstarch

¼ cup cold water

1. Place turkey in the slow cooker. Brush with coconut oil.

2. Mix together parsley, oregano, salt, pepper, and wine. Pour over turkey.

3. Top with mushrooms.

4. Cover and cook on Low for 7–8 hours or just until turkey is tender.

5. Remove turkey and keep warm.

6. Skim any fat from cooking juices.

7. In a saucepan over low heat combine cornstarch and water and mix until smooth. Gradually add cooking juices from the crock. Bring to a boil. Cook and stir 2 minutes until thickened.

8. Slice turkey and serve with sauce.

Vegetarian & Seafood

Quick-'N-Easy Meat-Free Lasagna

Rhonda Freed
Lowville, NY

Makes 6 servings
Prep Time: 10 minutes ⚬ *Cooking Time: 3–4 hours* ⚬ *Ideal slow-cooker size: 4-qt.*

28-oz. jar spaghetti sauce, your choice of flavors

6–7 uncooked lasagna noodles

2 cups shredded mozzarella cheese, divided

15 oz. ricotta cheese

¼ cup grated Parmesan cheese

1. Spread one-fourth of sauce in bottom of slow cooker.

2. Lay 2 noodles, broken into 1-inch pieces, over sauce.

3. In a bowl, mix together 1½ cups mozzarella cheese, the ricotta, and Parmesan cheeses.

4. Spoon half of cheese mixture onto noodles and spread out to edges.

5. Spoon in one-third of remaining sauce, and then 2 more broken noodles.

6. Spread remaining cheese mixture over top, then one-half the remaining sauce and all the remaining noodles.

7. Finish with remaining sauce.

8. Cover and cook on Low 3–4 hours, or until noodles are tender and cheeses are melted.

9. Add ½ cup mozzarella cheese and cook until cheese melts.

Two-Cheeses Macaroni

Mary Stauffer
Ephrata, PA
Ruth Ann Bender
Cochranville, PA
Esther Burkholder
Millerstown, PA

Makes 6 servings

Prep Time: 8–10 minutes ⚜ *Cooking Time: 2½ hours* ⚜ *Ideal slow-cooker size: 4- to 5-qt.*

1 stick (½ cup) butter, cut in pieces

2 cups uncooked macaroni

2 cups grated sharp cheese, divided

24 oz. small-curd cottage cheese

2½ cups boiling water

1. Place butter in bottom of slow cooker. Add uncooked macaroni, 1½ cups shredded cheese, and cottage cheese. Stir together until well mixed.

2. Pour boiling water over everything. Do not stir.

3. Cover and cook on High for 2 hours.

4. Stir. Sprinkle with remaining ½ cup grated cheese.

5. Allow dish to stand for 10–15 minutes before serving to allow sauce to thicken.

Cauliflower-Coconut "Alfredo"

Sue Hamilton, Benson, AZ

Makes 4 servings
Prep Time: 5 minutes   ❧   Cooking Time: 6 hours   ❧   Ideal slow-cooker size: 3-qt.

1-lb. bag of frozen cauliflower

13½-oz. can light coconut milk

½ cup diced onion

2 cloves garlic, minced

1 Tbsp. vegetable stock
concentrate

Salt and pepper to taste

1. Place the frozen cauliflower, coconut milk, onion, garlic, and the vegetable stock concentrate in your crock. Stir mixture to blend in the stock concentrate.

2. Cover and cook on Low for 6 hours.

3. Place cooked mixture in blender and process until smooth.

4. Add salt and pepper to taste.

Serving suggestion:
Serve over cooked pasta, cooked sliced potatoes, or any other vegetable.

Cheese Ravioli Casserole

Elizabeth Colucci
Lancaster, PA

Makes 4–6 servings
Prep Time: 30 minutes ⚬ *Cooking Time: 2½–3 hours* ⚬ *Ideal slow-cooker size: 3-qt.*

10-oz. pkg. cheese ravioli

16-oz. jar spaghetti sauce, with peppers, mushrooms, and onions, divided

½ cup Italian bread crumbs

1 cup mozzarella cheese

¼ cup Parmesan cheese, optional

½ cup cheddar cheese

1. Cook ravioli according to package directions. Drain.

2. Spoon enough spaghetti sauce into the slow cooker to cover the bottom. Place ravioli on top.

3. Cover with remaining sauce. Top with bread crumbs. Sprinkle with cheeses.

4. Stir to mix together well.

5. Cover and cook on Low 2½–3 hours, or until heated through, but without overcooking the pasta.

Veggies & Sides

Orange-Glazed Carrots

Cyndie Marrara, Port Matilda, PA

Makes 6 servings

Prep Time: 5–10 minutes ⚘ *Cooking Time: 3–4 hours* ⚘ *Ideal slow-cooker size: 3½-qt.*

32-oz. (2 lbs.) pkg. baby carrots

⅓ cup turbinado sugar

2–3 oranges, squeezed for juice to make approx. ½ cup juice

3 Tbsp. coconut oil, melted

¾ tsp. cinnamon

¼ tsp. nutmeg

2 Tbsp. cornstarch

¼ cup water

1. Combine all ingredients except cornstarch and water in the slow cooker.

2. Cover. Cook on Low 3–4 hours, until carrots are tender crisp.

3. Put carrots in serving dish and keep warm, reserving cooking juices. Put reserved juices in small saucepan. Bring to boil.

4. Mix cornstarch and water in small bowl until blended. Add to juices. Boil one minute or until thickened, stirring constantly.

5. Pour over carrots and serve.

Serving suggestion:
Sprinkle with crushed pecans and orange zest before serving.

Steamed Carrots

Dede Peterson, Rapid City, SD

Makes 4 servings

Prep Time: 15–20 minutes ⚮ *Cooking Time: 4–6 hours* ⚮ *Ideal slow-cooker size: 4-qt.*

8 large carrots, sliced diagonally

¼ cup water

2 Tbsp. coconut oil

1 tsp. turbinado sugar

¼ tsp. salt

1. Layer carrots in the slow cooker. Add water and coconut oil. Sprinkle with sugar and salt.

2. Cover and cook on Low 4–6 hours.

Corn on the Cob

Donna Conto, Saylorsburg, PA

Makes 3–4 servings
Prep Time: 10 minutes ⚭ *Cooking Time: 2–3 hours* ⚭ *Ideal slow-cooker size: 5- or 6-qt.*

6–8 ears of corn (in husk)
½ cup water

1. Remove silk from corn, as much as possible, but leave husks on.

2. Cut off ends of corn so ears can stand in the cooker.

3. Add water.

4. Cover. Cook on Low 2–3 hours.

Eggplant Italian

Melanie Thrower, McPherson, KS

Makes 6–8 servings

Prep Time: 30 minutes ⚜ *Cooking Time: 4 hours* ⚜ *Ideal slow-cooker size: 4- or 5-qt. oval*

2 eggplants

¼ cup Egg Beaters

24 oz. fat-free cottage cheese

¼ tsp. salt

black pepper to taste

14-oz. can tomato sauce

2–4 Tbsp. Italian seasoning, according to your taste preference

1. Peel eggplants and cut in ½-inch-thick slices. Soak in salt water for about 5 minutes to remove bitterness. Drain well.

2. Spray slow cooker with fat-free cooking spray.

3. Mix Egg Beaters, cottage cheese, salt, and pepper together in bowl.

4. Mix tomato sauce and Italian seasoning together in another bowl.

5. Spoon a thin layer of tomato sauce into bottom of slow cooker. Top with about one-third of eggplant slices, and then one-third of egg/cheese mixture, and finally one-third of remaining tomato sauce mixture.

6. Repeat those layers twice, ending with seasoned tomato sauce.

7. Cover. Cook on High 4 hours. Allow to rest 15 minutes before serving.

Mushrooms in Red Wine

Donna Lantgen, Chadron, NE

Makes 4 servings
Prep Time: 10 minutes ☙ *Baking Time: 4–6 hours* ☙ *Ideal slow-cooker size: 2-qt.*

1 lb. fresh mushrooms, cleaned
4 cloves garlic
¼ cup chopped onion
1 Tbsp. olive oil
1 cup red wine

1. Combine all ingredients in the slow cooker. Cook on Low 4–6 hours, or until done to your liking.

2. Serve as a side dish with your favorite meat.

Cabbage and Potatoes

Deb Kepiro, Strasburg, PA

Makes 4 servings

Prep Time: 15 minutes ⚶ *Cooking Time: 3–6 hours* ⚶ *Ideal slow-cooker size: 4-qt.*

I small head green cabbage, sliced thinly

14 small red-skinned potatoes, cut in 1-inch chunks

I small onion, diced

3 Tbsp. olive oil

2 Tbsp. balsamic vinegar

I tsp. kosher salt

½ tsp. black pepper

1. Put all ingredients in the slow cooker. Mix well.

2. Cover and cook on High for 3 hours, until potatoes are as tender as you like them.

Quick and Light Sweet Potato Wedges

MarJanita Geigley, Lancaster, PA

Makes 4 servings

Prep Time: 15 minutes ⚜ *Cooking Time: 3–5 hours* ⚜ *Ideal slow-cooker size: 3-qt.*

4 sweet potatoes, cut into wedges

2 Tbsp. olive oil

2 tsp. Italian seasoning

3 Tbsp. light Italian dressing

1 Tbsp. minced garlic

1. Combine all ingredients in sealable plastic bag and shake well.

2. Pour into the slow cooker and cook on Low for 3–5 hours.

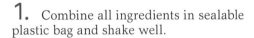

Serving suggestion:
To make a dipping sauce, mix together Greek yogurt, sriracha sauce, and minced garlic to taste.

Hometown Spanish Rice

Beverly Flatt-Getz, Warriors Mark, PA

Makes 6–8 servings
Prep Time: 20 minutes ⚜ *Cooking Time: 2–4 hours* ⚜ *Ideal slow-cooker size: 4-qt.*

1 large onion, chopped

1 bell pepper, chopped

1 lb. bacon, cooked, and broken into bite-sized pieces

2 cups cooked long-grain rice

28-oz. can low-sodium stewed tomatoes with juice

grated Parmesan cheese, optional

1. Sauté onion and pepper in a small nonstick frying pan until tender.

2. Spray interior of slow cooker with nonstick cooking spray.

3. Combine all ingredients in the slow cooker.

4. Cover and cook on Low 4 hours, or on High 2 hours, or until heated through.

5. Sprinkle with Parmesan cheese just before serving, if you wish.

Barbecued Baked Beans

Anne Nolt
Thompsontown, PA

Makes 6–8 servings
Prep Time: 15 minutes ☙ *Cooking Time: 3 hours* ☙ *Ideal slow-cooker size: 3-qt.*

6 slices uncooked bacon, cut into pieces

2 15-oz. cans pork and beans

1 tsp. dry mustard, or 1 Tbsp. prepared mustard

½ cup ketchup

¾ cup brown sugar

1. Brown bacon in a nonstick skillet until crispy. Drain.

2. Mix with all remaining ingredients in the slow cooker.

3. Cover and cook on High 3 hours. Remove cover during the last 30 minutes to allow some of the juice to cook off.

Creamy Vegetables

Gloria Frey
Lebanon, PA

Makes 4–5 servings
Prep Time: 5–10 minutes ⚘ *Cooking Time: 2½–3½ hours* ⚘ *Ideal slow-cooker size: 2- to 3-qt.*

16-oz. pkg. frozen broccoli and cauliflower

10¾-oz. can cream of mushroom soup

8-oz. carton spreadable garden vegetable cream cheese

1 cup seasoned croutons

1. Place frozen vegetables in slow cooker.

2. Put soup and cream cheese in a microwave-safe bowl. Microwave on High for 1 minute. Stir the soup and cheese together until smooth. Microwave for 30–60 seconds more if necessary to melt the two ingredients.

3. Pour cheesy soup over vegetables in slow cooker and mix well.

4. Cover and cook on Low 2½–3½ hours, or until vegetables are tender.

5. Thirty minutes before the end of the cooking time, sprinkle croutons over top. Continue to cook, uncovered.

Desserts & Beverages

Baked Apples

Marlene Weaver, Lititz, PA

Makes 4–6 servings
Prep Time: 10 minutes ⚬ *Cooking Time: 4 hours* ⚬ *Ideal slow-cooker size: 6-qt.*

2 Tbsp. raisins

¼ cup turbinado sugar

6–8 baking apples, cored

I tsp. cinnamon

2 Tbsp. coconut oil

½ cup water

1. Mix raisins and sugar; fill center of apples.

2. Sprinkle with cinnamon and dot with coconut oil.

3. Place in the slow cooker; add water.

4. Cover and cook on Low for 4 hours.

Peanut Butter Cake

Velma Sauder
Leola, PA

Makes 6 servings
Prep Time: 5–10 minutes ⚜ *Cooking Time: 2–3 hours* ⚜ *Ideal slow-cooker size: 4-qt.*

2 cups yellow cake mix

⅓ cup crunchy peanut butter

½ cup water

1. Combine all ingredients in electric mixer bowl. Beat with electric mixer about 2 minutes.

2. Pour batter into greased and floured baking-pan insert, designed to fit inside your slow cooker.

3. Place baking-pan insert into slow cooker. Cover with 8 paper towels.

4. Cover cooker. Cook on High 2–3 hours, or until toothpick inserted into center of cake comes out clean. About 30 minutes before the end of the cooking time, remove the cooker's lid, but keep the paper towels in place.

5. When cake is fully cooked, remove insert from slow cooker. Turn insert upside down on a serving plate and remove cake.

Dates in Cardamom Coffee Syrup

Margaret W. High, Lancaster, PA

Makes 12 servings

Prep Time: 15 minutes & Cooking Time: 7–8 hours & Ideal slow-cooker size: 3-qt.

2 cups pitted, whole, dried dates

2½ cups very strong, hot brewed coffee

2 Tbsp. turbinado sugar

15 whole green cardamom pods

4-inch cinnamon stick

plain Greek yogurt, for serving

1. Combine dates, coffee, sugar, cardamom, and cinnamon stick in the slow cooker.

2. Cover and cook on High for 1 hour. Remove lid and continue to cook on High for 6–7 hours until sauce has reduced.

3. Pour dates and sauce into container and chill in fridge.

4. To serve, put a scoop of Greek yogurt in a small dish and add a few dates on top. Drizzle with a little sauce.

Coconut Rice Pudding

Hope Comerford, Clinton Township, MI

Makes 6 servings

Prep Time: 5 minutes ⚭ *Cooking Time: 2½ hours* ⚭ *Ideal slow-cooker size: 5- or 6-qt.*

2½ cups low-fat milk

14-oz. can light coconut milk

½ cup turbinado sugar

1 cup arborio rice

1 stick cinnamon

1 cup dried cranberries, optional

1. Spray crock with nonstick spray.

2. In crock, whisk together the milk, coconut milk, and sugar.

3. Add in the rice and cinnamon stick.

4. Cover and cook on Low about 2–2½ hours, or until rice is tender and the pudding has thickened.

5. Remove cinnamon stick. If using cranberries, sprinkle on top of each bowl of Coconut Rice Pudding.

Best Bread Pudding

Betty B. Dennison
Grove City, PA

Makes 8–10 servings
Prep Time: 10 minutes ♣ Cooking Time: 2–3 hours ♣ Ideal slow-cooker size: 5-qt.

¾ cup brown sugar

6 slices raisin-and-cinnamon-
swirl bread, buttered and
cubed

4 eggs

1 qt. milk

1 ½ tsp. vanilla

½ tsp. lemon extract, optional

1. Spray interior of slow cooker with non-stick cooking spray.

2. Spread brown sugar in bottom of cooker. Add cubed bread. (Do not stir sugar and bread together.)

3. In a mixing bowl, beat eggs well. Beat in milk and vanilla, and lemon extract if you wish. Pour over bread.

4. Cover and cook on High 2–3 hours, or until pudding is no longer soupy. Do not stir. Brown sugar will form a sauce on the bottom.

5. When the pudding is finished, spoon it into a serving dish, drizzling the sauce over top of the bread.

Slow-Cooker Tapioca

Nancy W. Huber, Green Park, PA

Makes 12 servings
Prep Time: 10 minutes ⚶ Cooking Time: 3½ hours
Chilling Time: minimum 4 hours ⚶ Ideal slow-cooker size: 4-qt.

2 qts. fat-free milk

I cup small pearl tapioca

½ cup honey

4 eggs, beaten

I tsp. vanilla

fruit of choice, optional

1. Combine milk, tapioca, and honey in the slow cooker. Cook on High 3 hours.

2. Mix together eggs, vanilla, and a little hot milk from the slow cooker. Add to the slow cooker. Mix. Cook on High 20 more minutes.

3. Chill thoroughly, at least 4 hours. Serve with fruit.

Dark Chocolate Lava Cake

Hope Comerford, Clinton Township, MI

Makes 8 servings
Prep Time: 5–10 minutes ⚹ Cooking Time: 2–3 hours ⚹ Ideal slow-cooker size: 4-qt.

5 eggs

I cup dark cocoa powder

⅔ cup maple syrup

⅔ cup chopped dark chocolate, chopped into very fine pieces or shaved

1. Whisk the eggs together in a bowl and then slowly whisk in the remaining ingredients.

2. Spray the crock with nonstick spray.

3. Pour the egg/chocolate mixture into the crock.

4. Cover and cook on Low for 2–3 hours with some folded paper towel under the lid to collect condensation. It is done when the middle is set and bounces back up when touched.

Spicy Hot Cider

Michelle High
Fredericksburg, PA

Makes 16 servings
Prep Time: 5 minutes & *Cooking Time: 3 hours* & *Ideal slow-cooker size: 5-qt.*

1 gallon apple cider
4 cinnamon sticks
2 Tbsp. ground allspice
¼–½ cup brown sugar

1. Combine all ingredients in slow cooker. Begin with ¼ cup brown sugar. Stir to dissolve. If you'd like the cider to be sweeter, add more, up to ½ cup total.

2. Cover and cook on Low 3 hours.

3. Serve warm from the cooker.

Creamy Hot Chocolate

Deborah Heatwole
Waynesboro, GA

Makes 8 servings
Prep Time: 15 minutes ❧ *Cooking Time: 2–4 hours* ❧ *Ideal slow-cooker size: 3-qt.*

½ cup dry baking cocoa

14-oz. can sweetened condensed milk

⅛ tsp. salt

7½ cups water

1½ tsp. vanilla

24 or more, miniature marshmallows, optional

1. In slow cooker, combine dry cocoa, milk, and salt. Stir until smooth. Add water gradually, stirring until smooth.

2. Cover and cook on High 2 hours, or on Low 4 hours, or until very hot.

3. Just before serving, stir in vanilla.

4. Top each serving with 3 or more marshmallows, if you wish.

Tips:

1. To speed things up, heat the water before adding it to the chocolate mixture.

2. Keep hot chocolate warm on Low up to 4 hours in the slow cooker.

3. Add a mocha flavor by stirring in instant coffee in Step 3.

Metric Equivalent Measurements

If you're accustomed to using metric measurements, I don't want you to be inconvenienced by the imperial measurements I use in this book.

Use this handy chart, too, to figure out the size of the slow cooker you'll need for each recipe.

Weight (Dry Ingredients)

1 oz		30 g
4 oz	¼ lb	120 g
8 oz	½ lb	240 g
12 oz	¾ lb	360 g
16 oz	1 lb	480 g
32 oz	2 lb	960 g

Slow Cooker Sizes

1-quart	0.96 l
2-quart	1.92 l
3-quart	2.88 l
4-quart	3.84 l
5-quart	4.80 l
6-quart	5.76 l
7-quart	6.72 l
8-quart	7.68 l

Volume (Liquid Ingredients)

½ tsp.		2 ml
1 tsp.		5 ml
1 Tbsp.	½ fl oz	15 ml
2 Tbsp.	1 fl oz	30 ml
¼ cup	2 fl oz	60 ml
⅓ cup	3 fl oz	80 ml
½ cup	4 fl oz	120 ml
⅔ cup	5 fl oz	160 ml
¾ cup	6 fl oz	180 ml
1 cup	8 fl oz	240 ml
1 pt	16 fl oz	480 ml
1 qt	32 fl oz	960 ml

Length

¼ in	6 mm
½ in	13 mm
¾ in	19 mm
1 in	25 mm
6 in	15 cm
12 in	30 cm

Recipe and Ingredient Index

About the Author

Hope Comerford is a mom, wife, elementary music teacher, blogger, recipe developer, public speaker, ALM Zone Fitness Motivator, Young Living Essential Oils essential oil enthusiast/educator, and published author.

Growing up, Hope spent many hours in the kitchen with her Meme (grandmother), and her love for cooking grew from there. While working on her master's degree when her daughter was young, Hope turned to her slow cookers for some salvation and sanity. It was from there she began truly experimenting with recipes and quickly learned she had the ability to get a little more creative in the kitchen and develop her own recipes.

In 2010, Hope started her blog, *A Busy Mom's Slow Cooker Adventures*, to simply share the recipes she was making with her family and friends. She never imagined people all over the world would begin visiting her page and sharing her recipes with others as well. In 2013, Hope self-published her first cookbook, *Slow Cooker Recipes 10 Ingredients or Less and Gluten-Free*, and then later wrote *The Gluten-Free Slow Cooker*.

Hope is thrilled to be working with Fix-It and Forget-It and to be representing such an iconic line of cookbooks. She is excited to bring her creativity to the Fix-It and Forget-It brand. Hope lives in the city of Clinton Township, Michigan, near Metro Detroit, and is a Michigan native. She has been happily married to her husband and best friend, Justin, since 2008. Together they have two children, Ella and Gavin, who are her motivation, inspiration, and heart. In her spare time, Hope enjoys traveling, singing, cooking, reading books, spending time with friends and family, and relaxing.

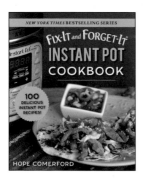